THE INSOMNIAC'S WEATHER REPORT

THE INSOMNIAC'S WEATHER REPORT

Jessica Goodfellow

ISOBAR
PRESS

First published in 2011 by Three Candles Press.

New edition published in 2014 by

Isobar Press
Sakura 2-21-23-202
Setagaya-ku
Tokyo 156-0053
Japan

http://isobarpress.com

ISBN 978-4-907359-07-2

ACKNOWLEDGMENTS

Grateful acknowledgment is made to the editors of the following publications in which many of these poems, sometimes in slightly different form, first appeared: *Beloit Poetry Journal, Best New Poets 2006, Burnside Review, DIAGRAM, Diner, 5 A.M., Harpur Palate, Hunger Mountain, Isotope, Literary Mama, Rattle, Reimagining Place, Verse Daily,* and *Yomimono.*

'The Beach at Big Salt,' 'How to Recognize Your Own Shadow,' 'Lagrange's Problem,' and 'Navigating by the Light of a Minor Planet' all appeared in the chapbook, *A Pilgrim's Guide to Chaos in the Heartland*, published by Concrete Wolf in 2006.

Cover image: *Fire at Full Moon*, 1933, by Paul Klee © Museum Folkwang, Essen.

Contents

Alphabet: Fugue:

for Naohiko

Uses of Water

WHY THE RIVER FLOWS AWAY FROM ITS SOURCE

All poems should be about water. Or bones.
And bones. Muscles like slingshots cradling knees.
Each step, wading through skin, sloshing.
A flood you cannot be lifted above.
Turning toward a longing for home.
A gold roof for the emperor. A blue roof for god.

Have you grown crooked as a plum tree,
or crooked as a black pine?
You will not know until you get there.
Your father, showing you bamboo,
its straightness, said, 'Each segment
has a beginning, an ending.' He was wrong.

Your mother, when your first piece
off the wheel listed like a weft-riven
spider's web, said, 'Never mind.
What is nearest perfection
is most easily broken.' You've never
made anything worth breaking.

See, there is no water in this poem.
There never was.

What You See If You Use Water as a Mirror

In Shinto, the eight elements
of beauty include impermanence
and perishability. Choose one
as your watermark. No,
that is the wrong one.

Begin by learning the 10,000 ways
to spell water. Puddle, swamp,
ice field: waters that don't
move. Estuary, geyser,
glacier: waters that do.

At lunch today, someone said
you were beautiful. The reader
is beautiful, he said. You weren't
there, but somewhere thinking
lagoon, waterfall, tide pool.

Knowing understatement is an element
of beauty, you thought drizzle,
fog, dew. All there is
to know about beauty can be learned
from water, so when you ask for

the other five elements, you are told
mystery, incompleteness, and – Wait:
to learn the final three is to dishonor
the previous two. You must choose.
But here's a clue: cove, tributary, sleet.

What You Wager if You Use Water as a Door

Sometimes the bodies are never recovered.
Once only an arm remained in the barrel.
Still, over half those who hazard Horseshoe Falls
bob to the surface below, gasping and flailing.
Mostly they survive their baptism by thrust.

To become the bullet in Russian roulette,
survivors say when asked why, though
some holler Fame, Fortune, or Political Protest.
As if a reason were needed. 2,632
cubic meters of water per second

obeying gravity speaks a primal language.
Listen closely. A river never lies,
even when falling. Nor tells the whole truth.
No matter how clear, water is still a door
not a window. Don't be fooled by your reflection

or its absence. Your body was a door prize, once.
If you lie down in trenches dredged by glaciers,
remember Ice Age. Forget newlyweds
who watch you crest and disappear,
clasping the bodies of their beloveds

as if that were the secret antidote to gravity.
St Niagara whispers, 'All doors are wounds.'
Which they are. A waterfall is a way to sieve body
from soul, temporarily, to try endlessness on.
A hinge on a hingeless door.

What You Measure If You Use Water as a Clock

The problem with the sundial
is in telling time at night.
How to know the hour
without consulting the sky –
the Egyptians were left
with only earth and water.

Earth begat the hourglass –
tangled eternity tipped upright
circular at each end
strangled in the center
the fulcrum of past and future –
because movement draws the eye.

Greek for 'water thief,'
clepsydra was the ancients' way
of heeding the passing hours
as water flowing into or leaking out
a vessel, a hole, a break in continuity.
The body is also a vessel.

But water will flow unevenly,
perfectly mimicking hours and years,
and sand can be sieved, finitely –
qualities of time best ignored by you
who, dust to dust, are seventy percent
water in the meantime.

All timepieces model pure motion,
the slide of earth round sun,
gravity's tug on water or sand.
All that convincing movement and yet
you only have need to tell time in the dark
if you believe the darkness ends.

How to Describe the Desert
Without Saying Water

Wanted: bauble of milky mouth.
Fat knee of shameless need, kneading.
Wanted: fontanel ticking, a fist
of collateral tightening. Frightening
whorl of faintest resemblance – thin
as glaze, angle, or desire.

What I wouldn't have (forsaken).
Crone whispered, Bridegroom hissed –
My groggy head in vespers once
northward canted. Cant = can't.
My fault. Crone's nostrums: always
it was water, variables afloat, science

listing. Crone intoned the Water Deva,
snake in the well. From feminine flotsam
infused a brooding brew. Awoke my desert(ed)
troth to sit unsheathed in a rainstorm.
The one constant was water – no planet
without it breathes. I was no planet.

And now. My moon blooms amphibian.
Glory, my taproot has plummeted.
My matrix is configured. Hosanna.
Madonna figure, de rigueur,
who once beleaguered be.
Full regalia my penetralia *is*.

Where You Draw the Line If You Use
Water as a Watershed

Coral blooms, a brain escaped to the seabed.
Soldierfish and damselfish – their clean colors inhuman,
not found in our dingy bones, our muddy blood.
In the iris, maybe. Of a stranger, perhaps.

Everything resembles the human body, or
doesn't. Even then I am reminded it doesn't.
These eyes I use to see with are locked
in their sockets, backdropped by gray matter.

This body I pack around, an oxygen tank's
antidote, will it ever be satisfied by the net
of comparison, dendrites filigreed
across synapses, sieving self from not-self.

But now my body begins its inborn origami,
folding an eyelid over the bright iris of the stranger
who floats in my womb while I float in the sea.
Now my body rejoices, finding a hinge

between self and not. A being to be, finally, adored.

The first lullaby in *The Singing Mother's Handbook*
is 'Can the Stars Be Edible?' Open your hymnal
and weep. Croon, lark, cantillate. Milk seeps, leaks,
smudges edges you thought skin had bound –
if loss is potable, why not stars? There are soups
of bird's nests, of rock lichens.
People sup on bee larvae, on sea urchin eggs –
the same people who wipe the dribble of clay
off a pregnant woman's lips and lead her away
from the river's loamy banks. 'But I want,'
she protests, 'to give my baby…' She falters. 'Spit,'
she is told and handed the songbook open
to 'How to Hold an Architecture of Rain.'
She flips the pages randomly past
'The Map of Sacred Things Just Out of Reach'
and 'Ten Ways All Lullabies are Forfeitures
are Good Practice.' She sighs.
'But there are no words to these songs. What use
is this handbook?' No use. No words.
Not for your resistance nor the tender way
it will be crushed.

What You Dampen If You Use
Water as a Boomerang

Between mother and son
the body as fact comes
sooner than between
mother and daughter.

I had not counted on this:
the polygon of bearing
sons, I did not know you
would hold it against me,

the body, for its lack
of edges, its fluidity.
I did not know you
could not move beyond a thing

without calling it [m]other. The sea
is not a boomerang, returning
unchanged – who boldly inked this
edge of continent on map? As if

blue roofs of ocean
shift and slap in maneuvers –
familiar and chaotic – the body
and its households recognize.

The Insomniac's Weather Report

CHANCE OF PRECIPITATION

Rain's tonal ticker tape
tarmac tarantella
rooftop timpani
water glitterati
articulate in triplicate.

River, all glissando
glossolalia
liquid limerick
wet tessellated
littoral lateral lullaby.

Ocean's hush-hush hoodoo
whispering womb
chez chartreuse chanteuse
fugue soothed in blue
a wish awash in white noise.

The insomniac longs to transliterate
rain into a human alphabet –
French, maybe. A lullaby, a chanson,
a hymn. A baptism of sleep
as unstable as water.

Rain

The insomniac flings pebbles at the clouds.
He says they won't stop following him.
        (If you keep secrets, you will drown.)

He howls obscenities into the wind.
He claims it goes right on talking about him.
        (If you fail to keep secrets, you will burn.)

No one can convince him otherwise.
No one is awake.
        (The patron saint of running water

Finally the rain runs itself dry
over the closed eyes of the insomniac
        is also the patron saint of silence.)

FLOOD

Mud-begotten, rock-ribbed, why continue to live on a floodplain?
Have you not wept to see your neighbor's hexed piano
floating in full grandeur down Main Street?
Did not your father also weep in nineteen hundred and fifty-four?

Have you not wept to see your neighbor's vexing piano,
mean reminder of $(n+1)$ nights it kept you wakened?
Did not your father also weep in nineteen hundred and fifty-four
though it was, then, a trombone – and a younger brother?

Mean remainder of $(n+1)$ nights it kept you wakened,
the thundering churn and thrust of the Broken Arrow River
though it was, then, a trombone and a younger brother
who were washed away and never seen again.

The wandering *Sturm und Drang* of the Spoken Sorrow River
is roaring louder than the startled cries of those
who were wished away and never seen again.
But familiar loss is desired above inconstant chance.

Warning louder are the darkled cries of those
who've made this mistake before. You reckon,
'A familiar loss is required in lieu of constant change,'
and so we all dwell in dangerous places.

Who's made this mistake before? You reckon
no one else. Anxiety sounds like an upright piano
and so we all dwell in dangerous places
like father's trombone-emptied basement, like the heart.

No one else's anxiety sounds like an uptight piano.
Mud begets rock-ribs. Continue to live on a floodplain – yes.
We *like* father's trombone-empty basement. We *like* the heart
floating in full grandeur down Main Street.

DROUGHT

Worse than (a road)
going nowhere
is (a bridge)
spanning nothing
but shrub skeletons
grass ashes
and broken
beer bottles.
Gumbo clay,
desiccated,
tessellated,
dried mud mosaic
under the
insomniac's boots.
The badlands
are bad for it,
mad for it,
anything defined
more by its *lack*
than not:
thirst,
debt,
futility.
Wind.
An excess of
Nothing.
So the insomniac
thought he'd
settle down here.
No better place not
to lay your head

at night, he said.
But the townspeople
(when there was a town)
the dirt farmers
(when there were farms)
the ranchers
the cowboys
the emigrants
the surveyors
the homesteaders
the claim locators
the tenant farmers
the railroad agents
the small landholders
were having none
of that.
Even the ghost
towns were having
none of that.
Enough of not
having enough,
they said.
Don't bring
your brand
of it here.
They'd spent
the day putting
down the last
of the animals,
kids hiding
in the root cellar.

They'd summed
up their accounts
and marveled
how many ways
the land could
betray them.
Or the wind.
Or the sky.
They were
looking for
a rainmaker,
a cloud lassoer,
a Midwestern Moses,
to part the dust
and bring them
water.
We look
to the night sky
for moon rings,
they told him,
not for dawn;
to the horizon
for clouds, not
clarity.
Waiting is all
the same, the
insomniac objected,
not a matter
of object
but of state.

Well then there's
the difference
between waiting
and wanting,
said the tall one,
tossing another
beer bottle over
the railing. Git
on now, cross
that bridge.
See if you can
come back.
Before I go,
said the insomniac,
tell me,
how can you
sleep?
Tell me,
came the answer,
how can
you go?

Fog

As fog is water
so the Holy Ghost
is God. One part oxygen,
two parts abyss.

Fog is the veil
of the unbetrothed sister
draped, at the well,
to beguile the suitor.

Desire is a blue
roof in the fog.
Clear days the insomniac
does not see it at all.

Fog exposes the air –
its stolen horizon
dropped at arm's length –
no other known suspect.

Holy, one part.
Sister, one part.
Desire and dread,
each one part.

To water there are three parts –
fog is four of them.

FROST

Of two minds is frost.
Only one that you can see. Or worse, can bear.
Don't ask the sleepless one what he has lost.

Appearing only briefly, like a ghost,
preferring to be every- or nowhere,
of two minds is frost.

Ice embossed on grass is easily chased
away. Like sleep. Like hope. And so beware –
Don't ask the sleepless one what he has lost.

A thing's edges and its center are star-crossed.
Sleep is broken by beauty briefer than a prayer.
Of two minds is frost.

To be crystallized at night comes at a cost.
You must cling to something colder than the air.
Don't ask the sleepless one what he has lost.

An insomniac by mistrust darkly is trussed.
He cannot choose: to disappear or to despair –
of two minds, as frost.
Don't ask the sleepless one what he has lost.

Snowstorm

All night the insomniac has watched it
falling evenly on the uneven earth –
a redundancy of snow unmapping the ground,
straightjacketing the quiescent trees.
The world, stashed in a magician's vast sleeve,
awaits the call of encore from its starry audience.

In a hazy pantomime of roofs and mailboxes,
snowing knit/purls to not snowing
like wakefulness to sleep: a slow raveling
or a sudden unhinging, the insomniac doesn't know.
He has failed to observe, again, how to truss
the self to the concussing of air, how to receive

the sacrament of sleep which, like snow,
falls in a mantle of colorless symmetric
absolution. The snow-saddled fence and his wife
under the coverlet are sine waves equally
swaddled in the nameless sameness
once banished to the runes of molecules.

Finally the self can stop talking to itself.

Tornado

bobbins of wind un-
spool houses people sleepless
eye warp without weft

unwind of people
eyeless bobbinhouses spool
outweft with warpsleep

eye spools sleep windless
bins of people bob warp out
weft with unhouses

The size of peas. Walnuts. Grapefruit. Hailstones are categorized (like tumors) after the bulk and heft of crops. Which is why the insomniac scooped one up and popped it into his mouth. It was better than he'd expected. He grabbed a whole handful and chewed. After that he didn't bother dusting them off first, scrambling to gather as many as he could before they melted. The final few he sucked to make last, pretending their slide into water was his idea.

He lay awake trying to say what about hailstones was so satisfying. Was it the way that (like manna) he couldn't store them up for the morrow? Or was it just how his jaw clenched when his teeth ground into them? In that case, why didn't ice cubes work (and they didn't)? A second storm hit. Pretty soon he developed a taste for hail and stopped longing for sleep. The Pennsylvania Dutch say eating hail prevents fevers, but it seemed to create one in the insomniac.

He studied the science of the frozen raindrops, batted about restlessly by updrafts till they become too heavy for the atmosphere and sink. He tried to make predictions, charting frequency (June the best month, with the shortest nights, the most storms). He moved around using historical data from the National Weather Service – Texas or Alabama in the winter, the Red River Valley in April, west to the Plains of eastern Colorado in July. In each new town, he'd drive around looking for houses with chicken wire screens on the west windows: people expecting hail.

He put ads in the classifieds of *Agricultural Digest*, offering to buy frozen specimens from farmers who'd save him hailstones in their freezers. These lacked a certain spontaneity and freshness, but he took what he could get. He tried various condiments – chocolate sauce, grenadine, ketchup – but always went back to the unadorned bone-shifting collision of teeth and ice. He developed a bit of a reputation, was thought to be a crackpot, or worse a scientist, but he didn't care. He was cured, though it wasn't clear if eating hailstones had made him light enough, or heavy enough, to sleep.

Flotsam and Jetsam

The Waters of Separation

Out-of-body travelers report an invisible red thread
anchoring soul to body, body to soul.
But if it's invisible, how do they know it's red?

My father said, 'There are five things
you must never forget.' Then he told me only four.
Keep secrets, even if you don't know what they are.

Wyeth's 'The commonplace is the thing, but it's hard to find'
= Heisenberg's 'Observing an object changes it.'
See everything, change yourself: which is not possible.

Don't worry about the fifth thing.
It's the same as the fourth, the third,
also the first. The second thing is wrong.

Nonetheless, welcome to your rescue.
Most things are invisible,
nothing is commonplace

= everything is commonplace.
Also, everything is louder
than everything else.

Lastly, burn cedar, hyssop, a red thread –
The invisible red thread?
I don't know. I wouldn't tell you if I did.

Kimono

Your dead mother's kimono fades in blue
chrysanthemum and shaded green leaf,
but you have only one word for both
dolorous colors. Never mind.
Many seaside dwellers draw no
line between watery hues,
unsurprised by the vagaries
of the salty kaleidoscope.
Shifts of light, angle, distance,
even wind can gust green
from the purest cerulean blue.
Time, too, is as fluid
as a noose. What's blue
doesn't stay blue any more
than what's past.
Every New Year you unfold
your mother's empty kimono.
Every morning you rise
on your island of Now,
surrounded by blue blue Time.

How to Recognize Your Own Shadow

My husband and I agree
on almost nothing. I told him
I would write this
in a poem. He said
I shouldn't.
Which was the correct response.

living in the pond out our window co-existing there are three
turtles two this morning on the narrow north end one on the
longer east bank all three are sunning are basking but no now
one northern turtle has backed into the pond submerging
himself among the murkiness shortly he reappears on the east
shore and the basking continues all morning he ferries himself
between the other two and I imagine them each calling to him
no one is more absent from me than you and the submerged one
answers *and no one from me more than me* but late afternoon I
see four turtles on the east bank and none on the north and all
are about the same size and now I can't tell which is who has
been where all day and now I don't know

People wonder why we stay
together. Only with myself
do I disagree more than I do
with him. I think the same
is true for my husband.
He says *It isn't.*

The Beach at Big Salt

Tools of antiquity – the compass, the straight edge –
could not square the circle, couldn't tame
its numberless sides. Arcs, curves, chords
of circles remain, tracing hollows of shells,
clawed waves, parabolas of sand. See
how matter curves around the emptiness,
how it cups and gently holds
the space where things are absent.
Matter buckles and spirals around it,
proving what is missing is more potent
than what isn't.

Matter aches to escape the discipline of being.
Creation longs to possess the freedom
from being a thing begotten. Even babies
in their mothers' wombs lie curled,
crouched around the swell of the primordial.
Straight or curved, tools cannot measure
what it means to be, after all this time,
still nascent, beholden to what
you can never know.
Armless, legless, a seahorse
unrolls his tail, reels it in endlessly
bobbing and straining in the tides.

The trouble with belief in endlessness is
it requires a belief in beginninglessness.
Consider friction, entropy, perpetual motion.

And the trouble with holding to both is that
belief in endlessness requires a certain hope
while belief in beginninglessness ends in the absence of hope.

Or maybe it's vice versa. Luckily,
belief in a thing is not the thing itself.
We can have the concept of origin, but no origin.

Here we are then: in a world where logic doesn't function,
or else emotions can't be trusted. Maybe both.
All known tools of navigation require an origin.

Otherwise, there is only endless relativity and then
what's the point of navigation, in a space where
it's hard to be lost, and even harder not to be?

Saying 'I don't want to be here' is not the same
as saying 'I want to not be here.' It rains
and it rains and it rains the things I haven't said.

Lagrange's Problem

By his fifth decade Lagrange no longer
reckoned celestial mechanics.
Already he'd wrestled the moon's libration,
why it veils but one face to show earth,
and 'The Problem of Three Bodies,'
the lover's triangle on which teeter
the earth, moon, and sun.

Lagrange courted equations, shunned intuition.
The slip of liquids, the shove of solids
he would not differentiate
choosing the dry elegance of algebra
over the earth's crude beauty.
Fluxion he distrusted;
only finite quantities spoke to him.
In his version of the calculus
the concept of vanishing vanished,
till there remained nowhere to hide.
Lagrange put down his pen.

Renouncing his efforts to quantify the night,
Lagrange edged into unknown variables.
All of France mourned. Marie Herself Antoinette
couldn't compel the sad genius to calculate.
The planets were no more and no less
perturbed in the slide of their orbits.

Of knowing, there is no end.
Or, there is an end.
One curse and its opposite,
also a curse.
Reasons to pray are the same
as reasons to forsake praying.

Happily the war summoned Lagrange,
duty over disgust.
For the first time in years
from his vast empty desk
he lifted his head and from his left ear
out tumbled *le système métrique.*
Thus the earth's disinherited
could measure their losses, at last,
in tenths, and tens, and powers of ten.

The Geometry of Being

3.1
When you call me irrational, you enumerate my offenses:
how I suck on sour candies till my tongue bleeds;
how I pile up the bills, unopened on the desk,
can't sleep for worry of the bad news they contain,
yet still don't open them;
how I say the opposite of what I mean
and am enraged when you don't notice.
Exhibits One through Three of my irrationality,
and Exhibit Four, you say, is how I smile while you enumerate.

3.14
Irrational numbers can't be written
as ratios of integers, finite fractions. Expressed in decimal form
they never reach an end, never reveal any patterns, never repeat.
I think of the ancient Greeks, how their word for irrational
            number
meant *measureless* number.

3.141
When you call me irrational, I hear that I am measureless,
that my emotions are. That is why I smile,
because I am, and they are,
or I wouldn't need to act these ways.

3.1415
Your last piece of evidence against me:
how I knew the lump was there for over a year,
how I felt it growing, but didn't tell anyone,
not my doctor, not my sisters, not you.

3.14159
My defense: I've been busy contemplating pi,
that famous and ancient irrational number,
the ratio of the circumference of a circle to its diameter,
the outer being to the inner being.

3.141592
Pi is a constant, the same for every circle.
Should I derive from this some comfort?
By arctangents, iterations, Monte Carlo methods,
to learn to calculate pi
is to know how to do what can't be done,
to learn how to be only by being so.

3.1415926
Perhaps a sacred message from the universe,
a number we may not deserve,
pi is a secret we learn one by one,
or don't learn
one by one.

3.14159265
Matter can be neither created nor destroyed;
to divide a curve by a straight line
is to force a comparison of unlikes,
to ask a question for which there is no answer
and no end to that answer.

3.141592653
Before you call me irrational
for things I fail to mention, cannot measure,

teach me the number pi.
Tell me, is it hopeful or hopeless,
this confluence of spirit and flesh.

3.14159265358979323846264338327950288419716939937510582097494459230781640628620899862803482534211706798214808651328230664709384460955058223172535940812848111745028410270193852110555964462294895493038196442881097566593344612847564823378678316527120190914564856692346034861045432664821339360726024914127372458700660631558817488152092096282925409171536436789259036001133053054882046652138414695194151160943305727036575959195309218611738193261179310511854807446237996274956735188575272489122793818301194912983367336244065664308602139494639522473719070217986094370277053921717629317675238467481846766940513200056812714526356082778577134275778960917363717872146844090122495343014654958537105079227968925892354201995611212902196086403441815981362977477130996051870721134999999837297804995105973173281609631859502445945534690830264252230825334468503526193118817101000313783875288658753320838142061717766914730359825349042875546873115956286388235378759375195778185778053217122680661300192787661119590921642019893809525720106548586327886593615338182796823030195203530185296899577362259941389124972177528347913151557485724245415069595082953311686172785588907509838175463746493931925506040092770167113900984882401285836160356370766010471018194295559619894676783744944825537977472684710404753464

Two Ways of Leaving

Here is the stone domed like a turtle
     for long life.
Here is the tree cut like a crane
     for good health.
Here are the moonbridge and the waterfall.

The road is four parts passage
six parts sky. Where you are going
may the ratios be favorable.
Let us paint pictures of bats
 and peaches for good luck.

The river is two parts passage
eight parts direction. It does not
bring back what it takes away.
Let us paint pictures of peaches
 and bats   black against the sky.

Poem for My Friends

I have no friends.
My friends have no friends.
On the way to a wedding
I don't want to attend
I pass a homeless person
scuffing along
and I think,
I could do that.
I need never go
to a wedding again.
My solutions are more drastic
than my problems.
All my friends are friendless.
They cannot be counted on.
I cannot be counted on.
Whatever it is I count,
there is always one missing.
Or two. Or more.
Or else there's an extra.
I cannot concentrate.
My friends cannot concentrate.
There is an underlying noise,
a whirring sound in this world.
It catches me off-guard,
though when I strain to hear it,
as I do now,
I cannot hear it.
My friends cannot hear it.
I have no friends.

Alphabet Fugue

Fugue: motion:

Beware the man who whispers in your ear
of birds. The secret to flying is no more
revealed from bird to bird than the wind
is passed from tree to tree. Little yellow birds
in particular are uncageable. They gather around
your feet, your gravity-riddled feet, proving
motion reveals not the particular that moves
but ~~its god~~ its opposite.

Fire too is a fugue of opposites, razing as many secrets
as it reveals in a blaze of form and discontent.
Later little yellow birds perch on blackened piles
of broken mirror melted clock eraser boomerang,
whispering, 'Beware the particular in the mirror.'
Isn't the opposite of a broken mirror everything else
broken? And the opposite of flying is not about motion
any more than whispering is about gravity, each a way

of being lured toward a center that isn't yours. Fire
is gravity's opposite. Only little birds escape
and then for no more than an alphabet's recitation.
The man who whispers in the ears of birds knows
how to draw you in with promises of flight and fire
as if they were the same, as if you had not already chosen,
watching motionless as your childhood home burned to the
                                                    ground.
In particular, beware: gravity is motion's ~~whisper weapon~~ god.

53

MOTION: MOON:

To remain in motion with gaze fixed
is like looking at the ~~mirror~~ Moon, orbit visible
but not spin, a lunar loop-the-loop
tracing the mathematics of attraction,
the dark gravity of desire.

In a second marriage no one wants
to be the ~~sacred~~ secondary body, a moon,
with little power to tender motion in other
bodies. I regret the stories I told you
had endings. Axis-lashed, you barely

blinked when I said that entropy wears
edible underwear. What I didn't mention:
absent atmosphere for light and sound to bed in,
Moon's skies are always dark and silent.
Moon's orbit too is loosening, its hoodoo

on Earth's oceans slowly waning. Secretly
each thinks the other is moon, moon is ~~god~~
~~mirror~~ other. No one names the *other* other:
Earth's moon does not revolve around it.
Rather Earth and Moon rotate as a coupling

yoked about a sun. A second marriage is a staring
match, two bodies in ~~a glass~~ a fugue so finely tuned
that neither ever turns its dark side to the other.
Tango of gravity, tangle of ~~ache~~ axis and sway around
a sun, a body nobody names aloud though it blazes.

Selenographia – a compulsion to map the pale
you cannot navigate. In particular, the Moon,
which is not, as whispered in antiquity, a ~~shadow~~
mirror of Earth, or of anything, in particular.
Also, not perfect, but furrowed as your beloved's brow
before offering you the usual bland expressions:
Mare Tranquillitatis, Mare Crisium, Lacus Doloris:
Sea of Tranquility, Sea of Storms, Lake of Sorrow.

Selenographia – glance of Moon as seen at no time
and more useful. An astronomer's map is fleshed
beneath a single illumination, fascination: each
feature rendered equally, mosaic of the Moon as never
seen ~~in troth~~ in reality, and more faithful. Like all maps,
more about the mapmaker than ~~the beloved~~ anything.
Mare Cognitum, Lacus Solitudinus, Sinus Medii:
Sea That Has Become Known, Lake of Solitude, Bay of the
                                                    Center.

Selenographia – from the edge of a spinning planet
astronomers used to render ~~anything~~ the Moon's face in part-
icular upside down, making each map as dizzy as the clock
that is the third strand in the fugue of our braided bodies.
Beloved, tonight the crescent moon is shadowed by the ~~whole~~
holy – old Moon cradled in the new Moon's arms.
Lacus Temporis, Lacus Hiemalis, Mare Marginis:
Lake of Time, Lake of Winter, Sea of the Edge.

MAP: GLASS:

A map of wind is usually called glass.
Subtract motion from wind, and ~~oh!~~ what's left
is window, map of subtracting self from ~~motion~~ ~~gravity~~
                                                    particulars.

An absence of glass is usually called shadow.
You'd thought it was the ~~opposite~~ lack of light, but no,
it's liquid dissolve of motion – you, trapped between god.

A map of self is usually called ~~whisper~~ ~~weapon~~ window.
Fusion of sand, lime, ash; ~~sacred~~ translucent barricade
against elements, motion. As if the self were other than.

A map of self is usually a window of ~~god~~ ~~gravity~~ smoke.
Childhood home burning, panes bursting outward.
Homeless, mapless, sparks rising like little yellow birds.

GLASS: TRAP:

Glass holds its breath in random
molecular scatter, in this way
more liquid than solid. Rigid,
uncrystallized, a trap for chaos,
which is itself a trap for self,
map for else. Or else its opposite.

The known ways to untrap the self –
sleep, sex, god, death – are also
the known ways to trap the self.
Luckily the self doesn't need a trap.
It is a trap, a glass trap, all liquid
ephemeral chaos, until you run into it

headlong. Constellation of scribbled
gibberish, lungful of gravity, translucent
truculent headstone. Call it what
you will: sacred scattershot, invisible
scar. A way of cooling a random
pattern, and holding it: your breath.

TRAP: FORM:

The beloved, reading your
manuscript, its many cross-outs,
laughs, looks up. Self is not
the only form, the beloved
says. Form is a trap, and an escape
from that trap. Other forms:
a poem, a window, a shadow,
a riddle, an equation, an orbit.
The body, you add, to show you follow.
In particular, a woman's body.
Not in particular, says the beloved,
frowning, turning away, inward.
In particular a body is a body.
A marriage though, two bodies,
that's a form.
Windows opening on
                              windows opening on

FORM: SHADOW:

A sacred property of glass is translucence.

An unlucky property of glass is translucence. Light's
entrance is also its exit: moon trapped in revolving door.

An unlucky property of breath is translucence. The visible
is easier to forgive. Early windows were thin sheets
of alabaster. Earlier still, shutters of dragonfly wings.

An unlucky property of breath is chaos.
Unlike wind, breath holds only itself – sometimes,
in winter, casting shadows. Wind casts matter
randomly. Breath casts only itself, randomly.

A sacred property of breath is chaos.
Slow leak from a body of faltering alchemy,
entropy's lottery. Haphazard light escapes
through the 10,000 gaps between breath and next
breath – invisible flute of fluke. All jelly and no fish.

A sacred property of shadow is chaos,
or rather, the absence of chaos – silhouette
of refusal, empty map of matter's insistence.
See how shadow crawls along the ground, seeking
a breach, a crack into which it will someday
drag matter, a place to hide the body.

An unappeasable property of shadow is form.
Denied the rite of translucence, matter calculates
its dark matrix. Collision of body and light –
what falls to the ground will not be trampled

barefoot. No matter; everything beloved is the same
as nothing beloved: godlike. Walk carefully –
your shoes are what you shine your shadow with.

SHADOW: DWELLING:

Dwelling in a foreign land, time is the only familiar
tableau, last locus. Even your shadow falls aslant here,
aping you strangely, or are you really hunched and scurrying
along the sidewalk? When did you grow so much
smaller? It is easy to become nostalgic. One easy thing.
Clearly time is not a landscape to make a home in.
Your beloved, in whose beloved city you now dwell,
agrees one of you has an advantage. But who? Remind
your beloved *dwell*, from Old English, meant *to lead
astray, to wander*. As *ravel* has twisted into *unravel*
and also its opposite. Meanwhile, your fingers twirl
a key ring. *Abide*, suggests your beloved, say you *abide* here,
remembering too late that *abide* echoes *to endure,
to tolerate, to bear*. Are all the words for holding still
so fraught? You both settle on *reside*, free
of overtones, swinging your legs over the balcony
that overlooks the park where you go sometimes
alone to feed the little yellow birds that remind you
of your childhood home. Neither you nor your beloved
suggests you claim to *live* here. Secretly you think
you dwell here, you are raveling, you are unraveling –
becoming opposite, and opposite's opposite. Only
your shadow lives here, still having everything
it has always had. Because your body is its roof.
Because you are its home. Its homeless home.

DWELLING: GRAVITY:

A man once told me
the best argument
in favor of
Marxism is gravity,
tethering you to
this parceled planet
as though an umbilical cord.
Escape is groundless –
jump and be yanked
back to this sphere
pocked and graven
with maps.

For gravity to matter
there must be
matter – two bodies
tending each to the other's
center. Having no
center might be a way
to elude the sacred
orbital. Birds in particular
are pale moments beloved
by centerless wind
whose map they trace
with hollow bones.

Gravity is a constant
reminder the body
governs not
itself and yet
strains to sway other
bodies, as in marriage,
perpetual stagger of desire
and resist, till exhausted
the body tends instead
to Earth's center, dragged
to its final dwelling,
its grave, by gravity.

Medieval cathedral glass is often thicker at base
than top. Not because glass is a river, a waterfall
tumbling in slow motion through the ages,
said the glazier who'd once been a priest. Gravity

is not to blame. Crown glass was hand-blown,
then spun. Who could expect a thrust, a whirl
from center outward to yield something faultless,
and level, and true. Consider the expanding universe.

An oeuvre is a body of work. Imagine that:
a body, not a mind, not a soul. A hand-blown *thing*,
matter wrapped around breath, and spun. Like a planet.
This the glazier offered as answer to the question

nobody asked: a journeyman one day
was hired to fashion an umbrella of glass.
Glass is a body, rigid but uncrystallized,
atoms spaced at random. It is chaos

that gives glass its transparence, but leaves it
easily shattered. Why not an umbrella out of glass:
a window on a stick, portable clarity; a chandelier
for the head; a whimsy for his oeuvre, his body.

So the journeyman molded chaos into refuge,
sanctum of shield and shine. Not unlike a myth.
Except a myth obscures as much as reveals,
and *umbra*, from the Latin, means *shade* or *shadow*,

while glass is ghostless. And heavier than expected,
more prone to gravity's lure, the body's *hamartia*. Holding it
he got so tired he dropped it. No – this is no myth,
let's be candid. He smashed it. I was that journey-

man said the glazier forgive me god
is in me like chaos is in glass.

BODY: MARRIAGE:

Most of a marriage is invisible, or more
precisely, not visible (compromise).
Like most of a body: dense, pulsing, nerve
and rheum held down by a spun skein of skin
                    (an opaque gravity, centered in periphery.)

What's visible can be mapped: wedlock,
tie the knot, conjugal bond, joined in holy
hymeneal rites. All maps are veined, even this one,
so that Hymenaois, god of marriage (compromise),
                    (was later named god of membranes.)

'Oh Hymen, Oh Hymenaios,' sang the ancients,
invoking by both names a god to twice bless a union.
From liquid breath flowed the much disputed (compromise)
                                    theory
that 'hymn' and the bloody window share a root.
                  (Which came first: the singing or smell of iron?)

Marriage is the form on which we break
each other, a sacred weapon, fugue of body and body,
violence of intimacy, or (compromise) vice versa.
Consider Beckett's 'the body, that scandal.' There is nothing
                                 about the body
               (you cannot say about the marriage.)

MARRIAGE: WHISPER:

There are infinite ways to say one
thing. Time and space are tools of one
god to name what is. Or isn't.
A compass needle spins like a second
hand. Like a child who keeps getting half-
life and afterlife confused, I did not mean
to remind you space and time are only two
ways of being alone.

There are no ways for me to say one
infinite thing about this marriage,
but infinite ways for you to say no-
thing, in two languages, infinity times two.
You force me to echolocation, like a bat,
a cave swiftlet, an oilbird – listening for
my own voice reflecting off your silence
in the darkness – to find you.

There is one word I hear you whisper
in the dark. Or no words. Whispering is one
escape, but from what? Never mind, in every
marriage is a whisper, throat's dark shadow,
secret convergence of regret and desire.
The marriage of time and space, for example,
whispers *Chaos*. My chaos beckons
yours with a whisper, breath friction.

WHISPER: BIRDS:

Beloved, from our rooftop I saw you
in the park whispering to the man
who whispers in your ear of birds.
What fugue of bone and wind
does he spin that you desire?

> Desire to map the alphabet
> of our mother tongue, syllables
> of our childhoods as intimate,
> as unteachable as a clock.

Why then do you whisper?
No one is around
save other birds.

> *(At this you look quite vexed.)*
>> We talk of anything,
>> of nothing. Of wind –
>> axis and refusal.

(After a hinged breath you add,)

> We talk of you. He's read your work.

In translation? In bird language?

> Does it matter? In both our languages,
> and neither.

Was it not, beloved, you
who claimed language matters first?

> *(Say my fears are as ungrounded as a bird...)*

Tell me the word for self
in your mother tongue.

> There is no word
> for self among us birds. No word
> for god. Or beloved. Or map.

A word for visible?

> Seventeen invisible words for visible.

And random?

                    In particular, for random,
                    but none for chaos.

Have birds a word for shine?

                    We do.

For desire, and bones? Why
won't you teach me?

                    A second language is a shadow
                    of a boomerang. Birds have no word
                    for gravity nor betrayal. You understand?

      (Now I am vexed.)

And still you won't explain
the need to whisper.

                    Because, *(whispers my beloved,)*
                    everybody's whisper sounds
                    more or less
                    the same.

BIRDS: LANGUAGE:

A general rule: small brown birds living near
the ground will tell you most. Wrens, sparrows,
blackbirds too have the most reliable voices.
But don't be fooled: from a single syrinx,
some species trill two notes at once, duet with self,
a fugue-less fugue, an alibi that leaves one set
of rooftop hieroglyphics, alphabet of birds.

If you beg the perching birds to be your confidants,
do you think secrets will come to you on wings? Ravens,
perhaps, will teach you *langue verte*, dialect divine, key to all
knowledge? Not if they know you mean to waste green words
questioning little yellow birds about whispers in the park.
Listen, vibration through bone renders your own voice to you
more sonorous than it is. Hollow-boned birds are not such fools.

What's more, yellow birds aren't ground feeders, not known
as truth-tellers. Could the Kabbalah, Norse mythology,
and alchemy all be wrong? Could Geronimo, St Francis,
and Solomon have been mistaken about *the oldest flying*
things on earth, trading gravity's obsession for a pivot on air?
Ask the dark-eyed junco (*Junco hyemalis (Hymenaios,*
hymen, human, hymn)). Ask anything dark-eyed and singing.

Ask the passerines, the passers-by. Ask and it shall be
as in the Ice Age, when humans followed birds
to find carrion. If you mistake a bird for an angel,
you will be dead a long long time. In the meantime,
carry on, converse with a god stain of feathers.
What flees you must have bone-hallowed wisdom.
What sings while fleeing shines its alphabet with scars.

LANGUAGE: BONES:

Language is a map of chaos, finely veined
in remembrance of the body, finally useless.
Language is the shadow of glass, which is nothing
like glass. In particular, string in the wind.
Those angels dancing on erasers in the corner,
do they praise the spoken word or the written,
the fusion, or confusion? Goddess of memory,
Mnemosyne, bore only daughters.
Or, bears only daughters –
hard to know which tense, what language,
to use with a goddess, with her daughters.
with memory. Language is imagination's gravity,
a failure more guaranteed than usual: using words
to describe language. Once you wondered
if cave art ever flung the moon as other
than calendar, spinning space instead of time.
Once you said light is gravity's imagination –
the give and take of light, it left you
hopeful. Forgive me: I have made a whistle
of your hollow bones before
you were quite done with them.

BONES: MEMORY:

Ivory piano keys, bone castanets, click
of ball-and-socket that should have swung
smoothly but didn't – this is how we learn bones
are for striking, for being struck. Reverberant tones
are what we call memory. What is cherished
for once having belonged to the body
is a relic. Click click. The body ossiferous
is a cave of punctuation. Staccato echoes require
labyrinth and rhythm, both found in bones, surprisingly
little more solid than thumb's pandemonium.

A skeleton is a form, and memory needs a form.
To last. To be last. It's why we collect bones,
recollect bones, build them a stone house
or burn them – solstice of vessel and memory,
each its own kind of resisting. Listen, *listen*:
whatever portion you collect, or recollect, is
by bitter definition, *the remains*. In this way,
you cannot fail. Nor fail to fail. The memory
of bones: if you cannot celebrate meaning,
celebrate form. The bones of memory: farewell,

meaning

MEMORY: SPECIES:

A species is not a perpetual motion machine,
drone of even numbers, string of quirks.
Or is it? Suppose your beloved,
who'd arrived mapless, mirrorless, visible
as the wind and tethered fiercely to nothing,
announces one day the death of a father
in the motherland. A father you'd assumed
long dead is only newly dead. You are
strangely grieved, aggrieved, as your beloved,
suitcase in hand, taxi waiting, leaves you
to your own lonely taxonomy. 2, 4, 6, eight –
even numbers repeat themselves,
like all species: a trap, its map and its shadow.

The newly dead are a different species;
the long dead are just like us. Whatever
becomes familiar is ruined the same way
even numbers begat nothing else.
Death's glare reveals anything as familiar
and stranger, your father, who told you 'Bones
don't lie,' did lie. Or you did. Everyone lies
about fathers, a reflex – part mother's milk,
part cleaver. Memory's boomerang careens
into your head, knocks you senseless. Sometimes
you rise more forgetful, sometimes handcuffed.
14, 16, eighteen, 20. A body remembers its species,
even if the mind wanders. A body betrays.

SPECIES: EMPTY:

If I mention 'perpetual motion' I mean 'a body leaning into the wind.'

When I say 'endless' I'm thinking 'if a species has a memory you are it.'

When I educate the air that I in patience wait for your return clearly I mean 'the little yellow birds of your childhood have lit upon my center but you are not among them.'

For 'absence' please substitute 'finally the birds will have a word for chaos.'

For 'empty' please hear 'a chronospecies is a species which changes physically morphologically genetically and/or behaviorally over time on an evolutionary scale such that the originating species and the species it becomes could not be classified as the same species had they existed at the same point in time. . . .'

If I whisper 'species' I mean 'a fugue of bone and clock and wind.'

For 'over time' please choose one of the following three: 'through a revolving door,' 'like a string of even numbers,' 'like a string of even numbers caught in a revolving door.'

Please erase 'an evolutionary scale' and insert a Möbius strip.

When I falter over 'could not be classified' it's because I'm busy pasting our wedding photo over that part of the definition.

The problem with 'had they existed' is that it suggests its opposite 'had they not existed' the way that 'memory' suggests 'absence.'

When I repeat 'the same point in time' I mean of course 'gravity may no longer be possible.'

I'm laying the last known strand of your hair down the center of this page.

If I howl pretend it's a dial tone.

When I answer 'No I've had no word' in every possible tense I mean it.

First Draft. Second Marriage. Third Person. Last Conversation.

One had wanted, even expected, upon hearing of the death of the other's father in the motherland, to attend the funeral, but the other had said No, there are some things that one does without another and this is one of those things. But why, one had asked, bewildered, and the other had looked pensive, not hurtful, though what the other had then said was in fact hurtful to one. The other compared it to how one had stopped showing first or early drafts of work to the other. One wanted to rebut but could not. One does not rebut the other when the other's father has just died in the motherland. Also, one knew the other believed it was jealousy over discussions of one's work with the man who whispers in the ear of birds that kept the first drafts hidden from the other. But there was not only one reason. There was another.

The other reason was that in fact one no longer had anything *but* first drafts. It was surprising and delightful in the beginning, and then it was devastating. For one thing one no longer had anything to share with the other, or rather one only had one thing to share with the other and when it was finished there wasn't any other until one created another. For another thing, one realized that it was not that one was getting to be a better writer and was no longer making mistakes; rather it was that one no longer saw any possibilities other than the one that was. There simply were no others. Whichever word came, it was the one. There was no other. Whatever happened was what was, and among choices there was no other. And this frightened one who did not, could not, tell the other.

The other was almost done packing the suitcase. One said one more time Please, meaning that one wished to go, to pay one's respects to the other's deceased father in the motherland. One has never met the father before, pointed out the other, and now was hardly the time. But there will be no other time, not after this, said one. This is the one time. And another thing, said the other, I don't know why one has been so jealous. The other was talking about the man who whispers in the ears of birds or else the other was talking about the father who had died in the motherland and one could not tell which was the one the other was talking about and which was the other the other wasn't talking about. And one felt that while one's world was shrinking to be simply what was, the other's world was expanding, widening, letting in more than just one and the other, but letting in another, a third person, and then a second third person.

It's quite ridiculous. He used to be a priest, one knows, the other said, picking up the suitcase and getting in the taxi. But one had not known that at all, not about the first third person nor about the second third person and so one still did not know which third person was the one who had been a priest. And so one did not know what one had been told one knew. And as the taxi pulled away it occurred to one that priest was another word for father. In some ways they were one word and in some ways they were one word and another word. And then one thought one understood, perhaps. And then the apartment was empty. And then there was no other.

For one day and then another and another the apartment was empty and there was no other. And so one decided to go to the park and talk by one's self to the man who whispers in the ears of birds. And so one went to the park, recalling to one's self that one had not seen the man who whispers in the ears of birds in the park for one week and then another and another. At the park one saw someone who was not one and was not the other and who was not the third person nor the second third person. The one one saw was a bird and one asked of the bird where the man who whispers in the ears of birds was, and the bird said that he had gone back to the motherland. But when had he gone back to the motherland asked one, and the bird said birds don't count the same way as humans and so the bird couldn't say but it wasn't one week ago it was another and another and even maybe another. And then one asked the bird if the man who whispers in the ear of birds had been a priest, or a father, or both, and the bird said there were no such words in the bird language and the bird flew away, and one yelled after the bird Chaos Chaos Chaos. And then the park was empty and one was alone. And there was no other.

THIRD PERSON: OR:

Either each human hair has its own spirit or it doesn't.

Either a spirit belonging to a hair, if it exists, recognizes the spirit of the body from which it flows or flowed or it doesn't or it doesn't exist.

Either the human hair on the bathroom floor belonged to you or it didn't.

Either the hair belonged to you before you left here or to someone sufficiently like you but not you. Like your father perhaps or someone else from the motherland who has hair with texture color and length similar to yours.

Either this human hair on the bathroom floor has a spirit that recognizes your spirit or it doesn't or it doesn't have a spirit.

Either this human hair fell from your head onto the bathroom floor or it fell from your belongings after falling from someone's head onto you or it fell from someone else's head onto the bathroom floor when I was not home.

Either this human hair has a spirit that recognizes yours or it has a spirit that recognizes a third person's or it has a spirit that doesn't recognize the spirit of the body from which it fell or it doesn't have a spirit.

Perhaps a human hair has a spirit which recognizes the spirit of the body from which it flows but once it is no longer attached to the body it no longer recognizes the spirit of the body from which it previously flowed. Perhaps the spirit of this hair once recognized your spirit or the spirit of someone else and no longer does, or perhaps it still recognizes the spirit of the body from which it flowed, yours or a third person's, or perhaps it doesn't have a spirit.

Either a hair is a long chain of amino acids, keratinized protein filaments, or it is a thing with its own spirit or it is both or it is neither.

Either I am imagining this hair or it is really here on the bathroom floor. You are not here. I am not imagining that you are not here because then I would stop doing that and imagine that you *were* here instead.

Either you flew away on purpose or you were taken away or you got lost or you went looking for the spirit of your missing hair which was here on the bathroom floor all the while, either with its spirit or without it. Or your missing hair doesn't have a spirit and you will keep searching for it indefinitely. Or you don't know your hair is missing and don't know what you are looking for, or you are looking for something missing which is neither your hair nor its spirit. Or this is not your hair and it has a spirit or it doesn't but it has nothing to do with your spirit or it does and that has nothing to do with you being missing or it does.

Either you know whether human hairs have spirits or you don't and either you left this hair here on the bathroom floor on purpose because you know or because you don't or you didn't leave this hair here, because of or despite your knowledge of hair and spirits, or you did leave it here but not on purpose or you did leave it here on purpose to taunt me or my spirit, if I have one.

Either you are coming back or you are not, and this hair is not saying and if this hair has a spirit it is not saying and if I have a spirit it does not recognize this hair nor the spirit of this hair, if it has one, and shouldn't I, if I have a spirit and if this is your hair.

OR: CLOCK:

Time is a perpetual motion machine. A clock
is not. A clock is a map of time that keeps running

into edges that don't exist. A human body
is a clock. A human mind says to itself,

'Today the moment I await will happen.
Or it won't.' Smacking into another edge.

The human mind is a digital rig, binary string,
while the human body is an analog clock, sweep

of perpetual second hand. Time, too, is analog.
This may be the secondary cause of all human misery.

Counting is a way of possessing. A clock
is a lock, a leak, a ruse, a roof of trees

on a hill, seamless and flowing as a tablecloth. A bird
plunges into the linen of leaves and is not seen

again. Wind, liquid as a second hand, as your body,
could turn up anywhere. When the trees are not busy

being bones of the wind, they dream a clockwork
of edges that don't exist, notched and geared and human.

Then the mind sings the wind for being mapless as
the body staggers headlong into wind's ragged edges.

CLOCK: RULES:

4:00   Don't expect one moment to be the same as the last. Don't think they are continuous, like a string. Or riven, like a string.

5:00   Do not feed your clock. No matter how it begs. A clock does not need nourishment. Nor can you expect it to give nourishment.

6:00   A clock is not a dwelling. Nothing can live there, not even ~~memory~~ language, which tries to live everywhere.

7:15   Your clock has an entrance but no exit. In this way it is like ~~a fugue a mirror~~ your childhood home. Before it burned to the ground, and was all exit, empty orbital.

8:00   Remember a clock is a trap you enter willingly. Like a ~~shadow~~ marriage.

9:00   A ~~god~~ clock is not a ~~clock~~ god. Even if you don't believe in ~~god~~ clocks.

10:40   Your clock does not know how to ~~whisper shine~~ count.

11:29   Your clock does not have good hearing. It confuses many similar-sounding words, for instance: fog, fugue, fatigue.

12:37   Do not use an invisible clock. It will tell lies, like a visible clock, but you will not know it.

1:22   A clock is not ~~gravity~~ sacred. It will claim to be, but anything that claims to be ~~gravity~~ sacred, isn't.

2:48   Your clock has deeply ingrained habits, such as turning clockwise, for example, or staying by your bedside. Don't confuse these habits with desire when they are, in fact, only habits.

3:21   What we call the face of the clock is not really a face. The hands are also not hands. We call the clock's components by body parts because we don't know the names for the parts of ~~chaos~~ desire.

RULES: WIND:

From the rooftop I see no one in the park,
no birds and no one whispering to birds.
Nothing except the wind – opposite
of gravity, shine of absence, everyday chaos.
A map of memory resembles nothing
as much as wind.

Like dropping my last coin into a bottomless well,
I whisper your name in the night. Wind, like memory,
has its own grammar: all objects, no subjects, no plurals.
What is 'losses' except 'loss' without an axis?
Wind counts backwards and forwards and is still
wind, doing nothing one by one by one.

For example, wind tugs at both ends
of this last strand of your hair my finger-
tips pinch like a hinge. A marriage is also
a hinge. A ransom, I let your last hair go
into the wind, into the ten thousand hands
that lose nothing or lose everything.

WIND: ROOF:

Pale knock at my door last night
I thought was wind and not
a ~~manlike~~ birdlike man ~~bird~~ –
three-piece suit of feathers
with mother-of-eggshell cufflinks.
He said he was your father.
I thought you were dead, I said.
Well, he winced, I have been.
He slouched like the moon
was his halo as he leaned
down to hand me what he called
your personal effects. In a ~~nest~~
paper bag. I took it in both
hands, light as a map. He asked for
a strand of hair. To match,
he explained, against
the remains. *Against.*

I showed him your hairbrush,
picked clean, and he nodded,
not surprised. Listen, said your father,
you may not want to hear this.
For some time I've been
nesting on your roof waiting for
the angels who dance on erasers
to come and do their hoodoo
in your corners. Over my shoulder
he glanced. I turned. There
they were, a pale blur of whirling
emptiness. Listen, he repeated,
back in the motherland – he gestured

with his ~~head~~ beak, as if to indicate
direction, as if it were his hands
full of your effects, his corners
being emptied. *Against.*

A flock of clocks flew overhead.
I stared at your father's one
brown boot, his one orange claw
below his pant legs. Loss
stitches you to this earth
like gravity, a kind of luck.
When there is nothing left
to lose, that's when –
He spoke, you understand, as if
~~a god~~ ~~a father~~ the wind.
I said nothing. I said *Against.*

Your father cleared his ~~throat~~ duet-
singing syrinx and said, When
the angels have fled, leaving
their erasers behind, then
you can erase yourself
a roof. I have a roof, I said.
Your father's beak turned down.
Humans are one of the few
mammals that see colors,
like birds do. Answer my question
and I'll rewind the clock,
the wind. I'll flee with the angels
from your roof. His riddle:
What color are the angels?

I looked, but what color is
emptiness, perpetual whirl of
nothing, wind. I turned
but your father
had vanished. Here
is what was in the bag:
yellow feathers that combusted
when I put them in my mouth.
Against my mouth.

fugue

1597, from It. *fuga*, lit. 'flight,' from L. *fuga* 'act of fleeing,' from *fugere* 'to flee' (see **fugitive**). Current spelling is from influence of Fr. version of the It. word. Defined in Elson's Music Dictionary as 'a composition in strict style, in which one subject is proposed by one part and answered by other parts, according to certain rules.'

According to certain rules, I erased myself
a roof. A random roof, liquid awning,
canopy beneath the flight of birds and god.
Roof like a glass umbrella, like a myth.

According to certain rules, guardians of your flight
settled on my erased eaves like it was
a Chinese roof. Through glassy fascia
I see them, each one facing southeast.

Dancing among them: your father, errant angels,
the man who whispers in the ears of birds
(who may also be your father), all of them
up there on the roof I erased myself,

according to certain rules. Their heels tap
out 'fugitive' in Morse code, like the click
click of bones, odes on missing erasers.
You were my ~~roof~~ eraser. According to certain rules.

Main Entry: **fugue**
Function: *noun*
Etymology: probably from Italian *fuga* flight, fugue, from
        Latin, flight, from *fugere*
Date: 1597

1 a : a musical composition in which one or two themes are
repeated or imitated by successively entering voices and con-
trapuntally developed in a continuous interweaving of the voice
parts **b :** something that resembles a fugue especially in inter-
weaving repetitive elements
2 : a disturbed state of consciousness in which the one affected
seems to perform acts in full awareness but upon recovery cannot
recollect the acts performed

> The acts performed include gamboling
> over the gables as they turn out their pockets,
> searching for misplaced erasers. Who knew
> even angels could lose their tools of trade, flee
> and boomerang, and forget? One of them
> two-steps with your father, one of your fathers.
>
> The acts performed include taxiing, not calling,
> not appearing. A chorus of interwoven
> voices not entering, successively, like a bird
> who can sing harmony with itself, one-part
> fugue. Leaving one hair on the bathroom floor
> facing southeast. Or not leaving it.
>
> The acts performed include ordinary chaos:
> marrying, burying, burning, biding, losing track

of fathers, spouses, memory, the only flagellant
left. For each who flees, one remains, inventing
the place where god and not-god overlap like
shingles on the roof where I erased myself.

fugue *n.* **1** a musical composition on one or more short subjects,
which are repeated by successively entering voices and developed
contrapuntally.   **2** (*Psych.*) an attempt to escape from reality.   **3**
(*Psych.*) loss of memory coupled with disappearance from one's
usual environments.

One's usual environments include this city,
fugue of roofs under eye-strung stars,
warped and wrapped in gravity,
god-friction, the opposite of wind.
It's a short subject, usual environments:
fugue of string, shadow, and clock.

Escape is a long subject, long shadow
falling on the roof that's left behind.
Autumn leaves in fugue sing their alto
colors until one by one breathless
they become ransom notes that clog
your gutters, IOUs from gravity, wind, death.

Wind is not an environment – this all fugitives
learn, all autumn leaves, all who breathless
sing the marriage fugue. One's usual environments
are more or less what ~~disappears~~ dwell beneath
the roofs of everyday chaos coupled with
time, starting and stopping fitfully, like ~~memory~~ wind.

fugue

NOUN: **1.** *Music* An imitative polyphonic composition in which a theme or themes are stated successively in all of the voices of the contrapuntal structure. **2.** *Psychiatry* A pathological amnesiac condition during which one is apparently conscious of one's actions but has no recollection of them after returning to a normal state. This condition, usually resulting from severe mental stress, may persist for as long as several months.

For as long as several months what can be endured
includes absence, shadow, desire and its chaos,
the fugue of not knowing, imagination's tarantella.
The rule of even numbers states that entrance equals
exit – a senseless phrase, 'equal but opposite.'
Everything equal is opposite. Nothing opposite is disaster.

For as long as several months little yellow birds
outlined the blackened roof. Your small self supposed
one to be the soul of your father, never exhaling until
the last had flown away. When you sifted through the ashes,
exactly zero bones were found – this you never
told me. When you could no longer keep your father

dead, I could no longer keep you. A makeweight
standing in for makepeace, counterbalance heaving
gravity bearable. Forgive me: what I'd thought
was axis was bone. The click of your key in the lock
is the click of my faltering knees at the altar
of married love, an alphabet in the dark.

FUGUE: DESIRE:

If the world is a suitcase and not a souvenir.
If there are rules for desire, eye of the needle.
If winter identifies herself by the act of emptying,
baptizing roof after roof like each was a fontanel.
If I heard your key in lock. *If* you walked in,
census taker of the underworld, suitcase in hand,
would you notice my emptied-out corners, our missing
roof? Or would we rush to sing a fugue of pronouns,
to intone other words so we didn't say ~~betrayal~~ absence.

What is a fugue anyway, but talking all at once,
saying the same things, drowning out the click
click of bones with jaw-hinged clicking, long white
fugue of entrances and exits, autumn waiting for
winter, dull edge of desire. *If* there is nothing more
perfect than a stranger. *If* horizon is a hinge
between earth and sky, what is desire? *If* I can no more
keep your absence than I could keep you.
So begins, click click, our third marriage.

DESIRE: AGAINST:

River shoulders boat the way Atlas shores up world.
Such a precarious world.

River bears boat like mourner offering coffin skyward.
Such a reluctant tumbrel.

River balances boat like woman swaying under water jug, willing
        water homeward.
Such a vagrant horizon.

Source of River is like any other source, left ever farther behind.
        One-way River.
Still Source is River's one-and-only; boat is not.

Mouth of River is like every other mouth, finally rinsed with silt,
mother tongue clay-clogged.

River at mouth burbles, 'I made a pact with myself not to be
        here when I got back.'
Boat has no choice.

I do not think gravity ~~is a revolving door~~ is an eraser.
I do ~~not~~ think a revolving door is ~~an eraser is~~ language.
I do not not think an eraser is language ~~is a species~~.
I ~~do not~~ think language is ~~a species is~~ memory.
I do not think a species ~~is memory~~ is a clock.
I do not not think memory is ~~a clock is~~ desire.
I do not think a clock ~~is desire~~ is a map.
I do ~~not not~~ think desire is a map ~~is a roof~~.
I do not think a map is ~~a roof is~~ an alphabet.
I do not think a roof ~~is an alphabet~~ is a fugue.
~~I do not think~~ an alphabet is a fugue ~~is bones~~.
I do not not think a fugue is ~~bones are~~ a perpetual motion
     machine.
I do not think bones are ~~a perpetual motion machine is~~ a
     dwelling.
I do not think a perpetual motion machine is ~~a dwelling is~~
     escape.
I do ~~not~~ think dwelling is escape ~~is an axis~~.
I do not think escape ~~is an axis~~ is god.
I ~~do not~~ think an axis ~~is god~~ is counting.
I do not think god is counting chaos.
I do ~~not~~ think counting is ~~chaos is~~ breath.
I do ~~not not~~ think chaos ~~is breath~~ is absence.
I ~~do not~~ think breath is ~~absence is~~ a boomerang.
I do ~~not~~ think absence is ~~a boomerang is~~ gravity.
I do not think a boomerang is ~~gravity is~~ a revolving door.
I do not think gravity is ~~a revolving door is~~ an eraser.

In particular, chaos – its horizontal alphabet,
its third-person motion –
I remember. What cannot be
recalled must riddle
body's tender axis.
For example, erase this:
function of night sky –
to make our bodies crave
the curve of earth
as if it were a choice.

MEMORY: ALPHABET:

Struck in the chest with absence's boomerang,
gravity's revolving door like a breath. Desire
is an alphabet unto itself. Desire is space
shuffling. Longing is a hinge, an axis of still-
ness while all else flails, part particle, part madness.

Write it down so you remember: writing
is not memory. Don't confuse what the body
ekes with the sacred, what it leaks with meaning.
The cartographer's question: is it more divine to render
the visible invisible, or vice versa? Landmark or latitude?

Meanwhile, the man who whispers in the ears of birds
breathes a green alphabet. Many colors speak
to each other but green talks only to itself,
like the body waiting for the mind's
recognition. And waiting. You must never

utter, 'All is lost.' Always there is more
that could vanish or be taken. When you are certain
your bones have been flayed hollow, then you might forget:
memory's last bastion could dissolve between neurons.
And still, you could lose more: you could remember.

ALPHABET: FUGUE:

An alphabet is a vessel for
Chaos, also the name of god's
pet yellow bird in every known
alphabet. Memory is a cage
for the cageless, a Möbius-strip
umbilical cord, a vessel for what
the alphabet does in the dark. Loss
is the only souvenir. A shadow
is a vessel of nothing – that's why
remembering tethers itself to darkness,
either the absence of shadow or all
shadow. If *the eye is the first circle*,
then memory is the broken circle, door
hung on a crooked hinge, leaking
light.

Memory's dalliance with light
is treacherous to the act of
remembering. Light, always a vessel
of something, breaks promises never
made. Therefore, beloved, you
and I, each with our own pocket
god, our exquisitely useless
alphabets that keep nothing
from vanishing again and again,
let us remember that chance
is our only chance. Let us sing an alphabet
fugue, best done with our mouths
clamped shut, shadows leading,
yellow birds flying overhead,
circling.

Notes & Thanks

WHAT YOU SEE IF YOU USE WATER AS A MIRROR: The three elements of beauty not listed in the poem are appreciation of age, imperfection, and simplicity. Some sources cite a ninth element: irregularity.

WHAT YOU OVERLOOK IF YOU USE WATER AS A COMPASS: The italicized line is from the *Tao Te Ching*.

KIMONO: Traditionally the Japanese language had only one word, *ao*, for both blue and green. During the Heian Period, a word for green, *midori*, came into usage, although it was considered a shade of blue rather than its own color. During the post-World War II occupation of Japan, influence from the West promoted a clear distinction between blue and green, though even today some kinds of vegetation are still called *aoi* (adjective form), and green stoplights are said to be 'blue.' Most other green objects are nowadays referred to as *midori*. This grouping of blue and green into one category is common in many other cultures as well.

LAGRANGE'S PROBLEM: This poem is based on the life of mathematician Joseph-Louis Lagrange (1736-1813). His work in many diverse fields of mathematics might have allowed him to be numbered with the greatest mathematicians of all time, had melancholy not derailed his brilliant career on several occasions.

THE GEOMETRY OF BEING: The italicized phrase is from Richard Preston.

BIRDS: LANGUAGE: Italicized lines in the first stanza are either quotes or paraphrases from Alexia Stevens at NatureSkills.com.

The phrase 'the oldest flying things on earth' is borrowed from Richard Powers' description of sandhill cranes.

SPECIES: EMPTY: The definition of chronospecies comes from Wikipedia, retrieved September 7, 2010, from http://en.wiki pedia.org/wiki/Chronospecies. The absence of commas in the definition is my intentional omission.

ROOF: FUGUE: Definitions, in the order they appear in the poem, are from:

1. *Online Etymology Dictionary*, Retrieved August 31, 2008, from www.etymonline.com/index/php?search=fugue&search mode=none
2. *The Merriam-Webster Online Dictionary*, Retrieved August 31, 2008, from www.merriam-webster.com/dictionary/fugue
3. *The Cassell Concise Dictionary* (1997)
4. *The American Heritage Dictionary of the English Language: Fourth Edition* (2000), Retrieved August 31, 2008, from www.bartleby.com/61/24/F0352400.html

ALPHABET: FUGUE: The italicized phrase is from Ralph Waldo Emerson's *Essays: First Series*, 'Circles' (1841).

The Insomniac's Weather Report won the Three Candles Press First Book Award in 2011; heartfelt thanks to Steve Mueske of Three Candles Press, and Alexander Long, who judged the competition. Sincere appreciation for the insights of Michele Battiste of the Dzanc Creative Writing Sessions.

My deep gratitude for endless encouragement and support goes to: Lana Hechtman Ayers, Shannon Borg, Lydia Dishman, Judy Halebsky, Kerry Hudson, Erin Malone, and Tracy Slater. For all things, love and thanks to Naohiko, Taiyo, and Hugo Ueno.